I0816401

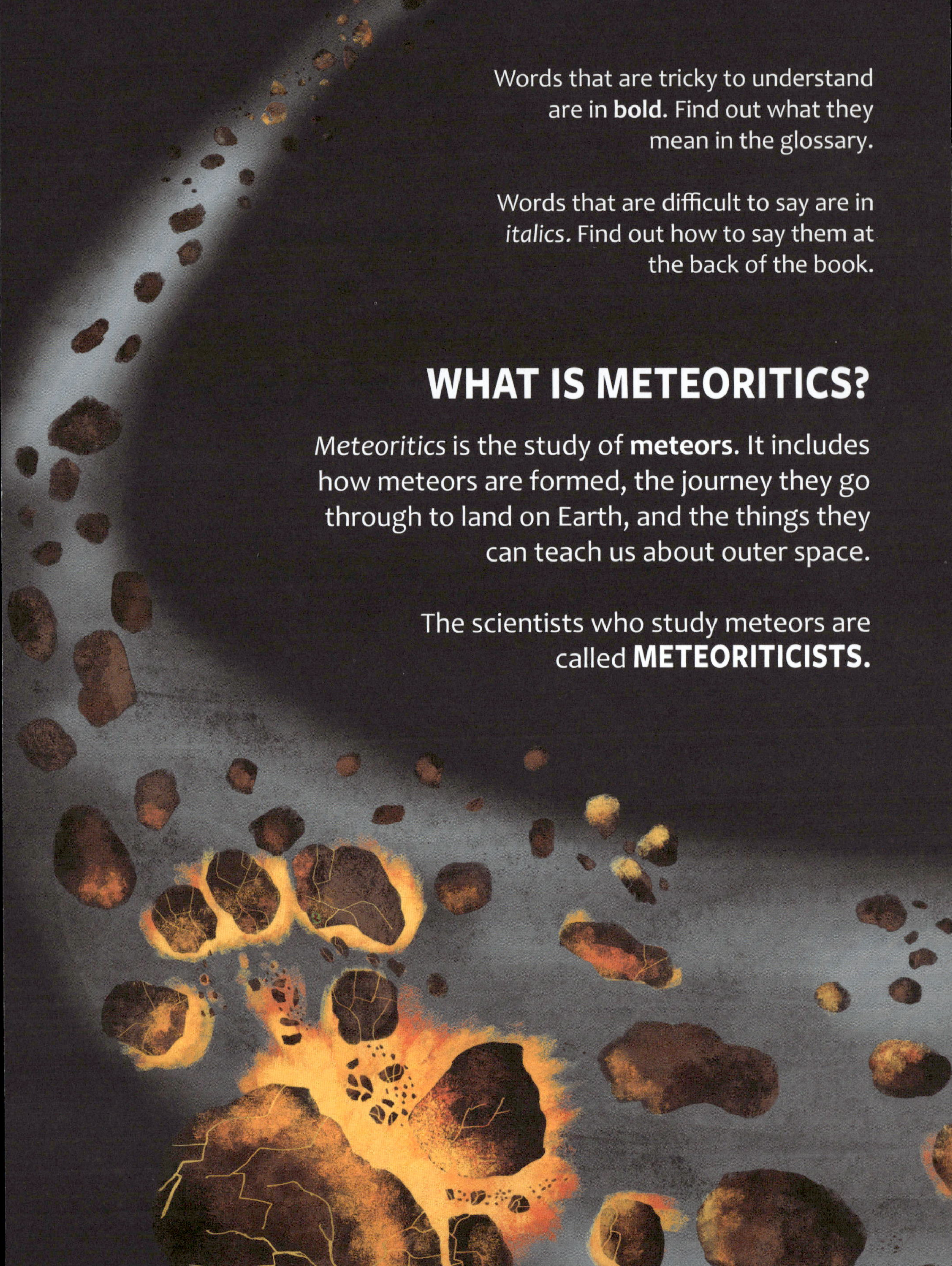

Words that are tricky to understand are in **bold**. Find out what they mean in the glossary.

Words that are difficult to say are in *italics*. Find out how to say them at the back of the book.

WHAT IS METEORITICS?

Meteoritics is the study of **meteors**. It includes how meteors are formed, the journey they go through to land on Earth, and the things they can teach us about outer space.

The scientists who study meteors are called **METEORITICISTS.**

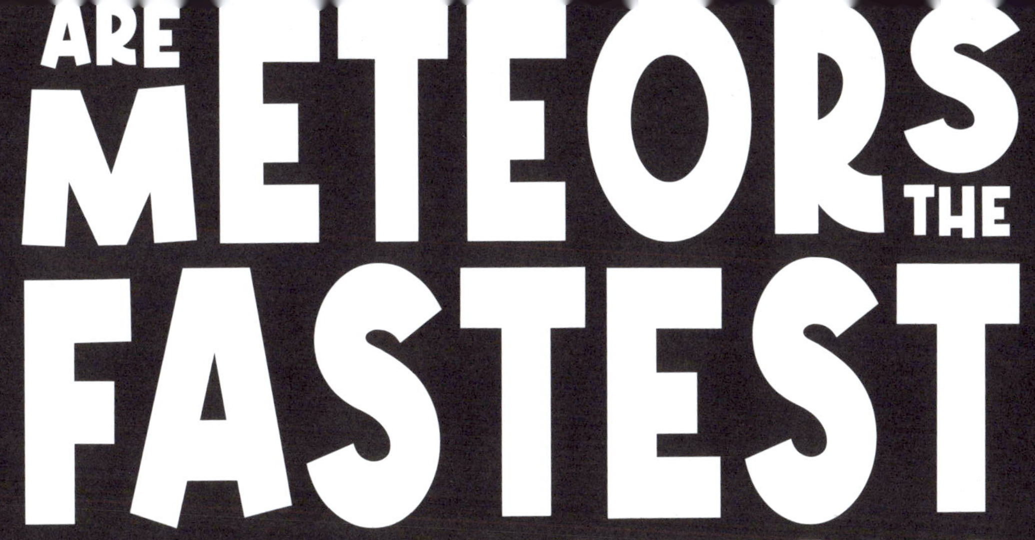

ARE METEORS THE FASTEST THINGS IN OUTER SPACE?

DISCOVER THE SCIENCE BEHIND **METEORITICS**
(ME-tee-or-IT-iks)

Written by Rosie Rowntree
Illustrated by Verónika Cháves Morales

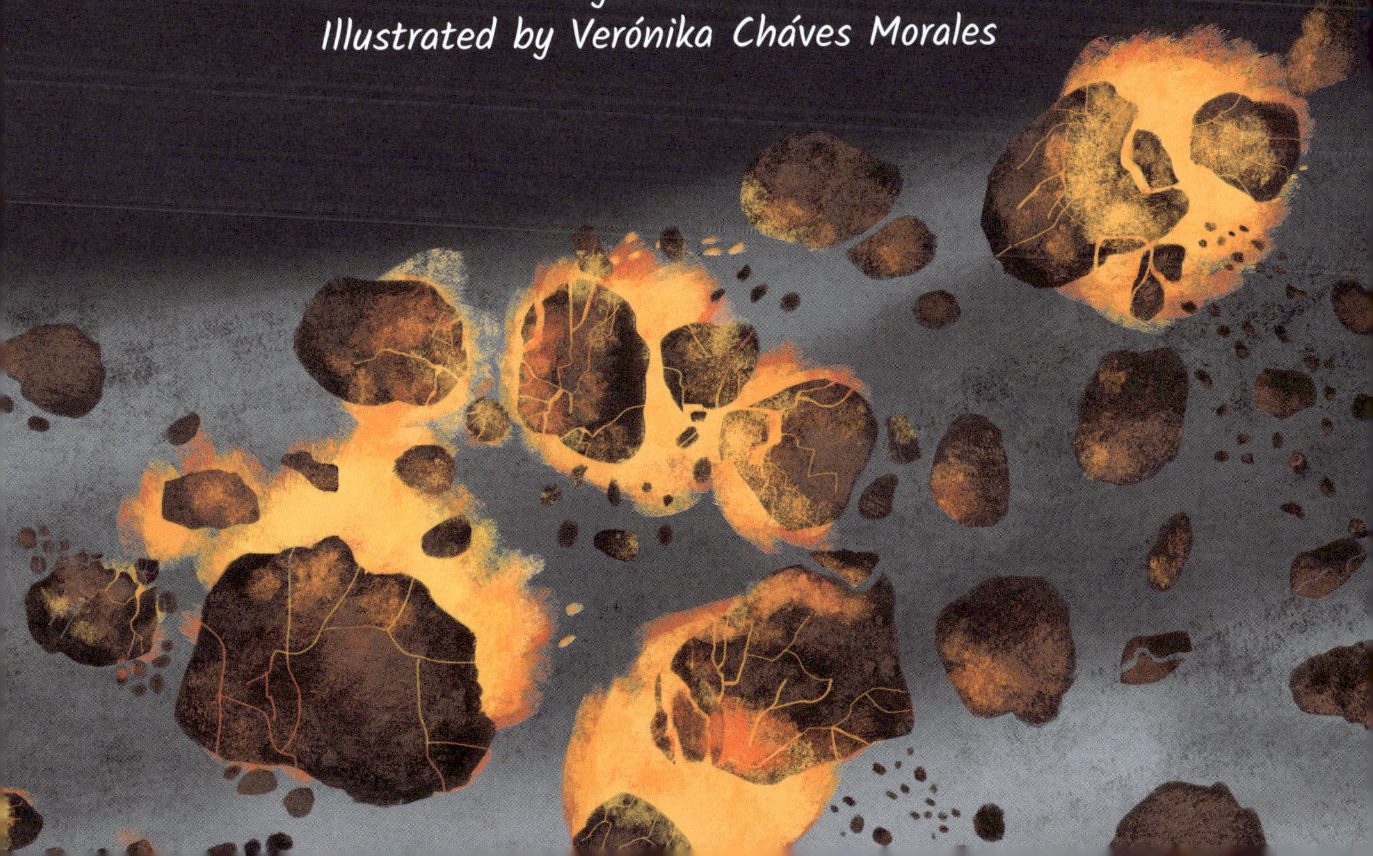

In November 1833, people living across North America woke up in the middle of the night to find their bedrooms filling with light.

They rushed outside and, to their amazement, saw hundreds of thousands of bright streaks racing across the sky.

People called it "the night the stars fell". Scientists we would now call *meteoriticists* knew that it was a **meteor shower.** It was one of the most **spectacular in history!**

Meteors are rocks falling from space. They can be as tiny as a piece of dust or as big as a car.

Most meteors start their journey through space as part of an **asteroid** in the **asteroid belt** between Mars and Jupiter.

Asteroids are rocky objects left over from when the **solar system** was formed billions of years ago. When they crash into each other, small pieces called **meteoroids** break off!

When meteoroids fall to Earth, they turn into meteors. They travel very quickly through the **atmosphere**, pulled down toward the surface by Earth's **gravity**.

The fastest meteors can travel at 158,000 **mph** (255,000 **kph**). That's like being able to fly all the way around Earth's **equator** in less than ten minutes. The fastest plane ever built would take over five hours!

When high-speed meteors collide with the thick air in
Earth's atmosphere, they heat up the **gases** around them
so much that they **start to glow!**

They also leave a long trail of light behind them. This is why they are nicknamed "shooting **stars**" – even though they're not actually stars at all!

Meteoriticists use these trails of light to calculate how fast the meteors are going and what direction they are moving in. While most meteors are destroyed in the atmosphere because of the intense heat, some survive.

Meteoriticists call these pieces of rock that land on Earth **meteorites**. They can be collected and studied!

Meteorites are one of very few things from outer space that scientists can touch.

Because they were originally part of asteroids billions of years old, meteorites can teach us a lot about the history of our solar system and how the planets were formed!

The Moon shows what happens when meteorites hit solid ground very quickly. Its surface is covered in **craters** created by meteorite impacts. The Moon's very thin atmosphere doesn't provide much protection, so meteorites hit the surface with **a lot of energy!**

If humans ever build a Moon base, it would need to be well **shielded** to protect the people living and working inside.

On Earth the chances of being hit by one meteorite – let alone two or more – are extremely small. Unlike the Moon, Earth's thick atmosphere breaks up most meteors before they do any damage.

In fact, there is only one case in recorded history of a person being hit by a meteorite – and thankfully they survived!

Despite the incredible speed that meteors travel at, they are still not the fastest things in the solar system!

Mercury is faster. It is the closest planet to the Sun and uses the intense pull of our star's gravity to complete one full **orbit** in just 88 days. It takes Earth 365 days.

Some speedy things built by humans can overtake meteors too! While on a mission to study the Sun, the Parker Solar Probe reached an amazing top speed of 430,000 mph (692,000 kph)! That's nearly **three times faster than the quickest meteors!**

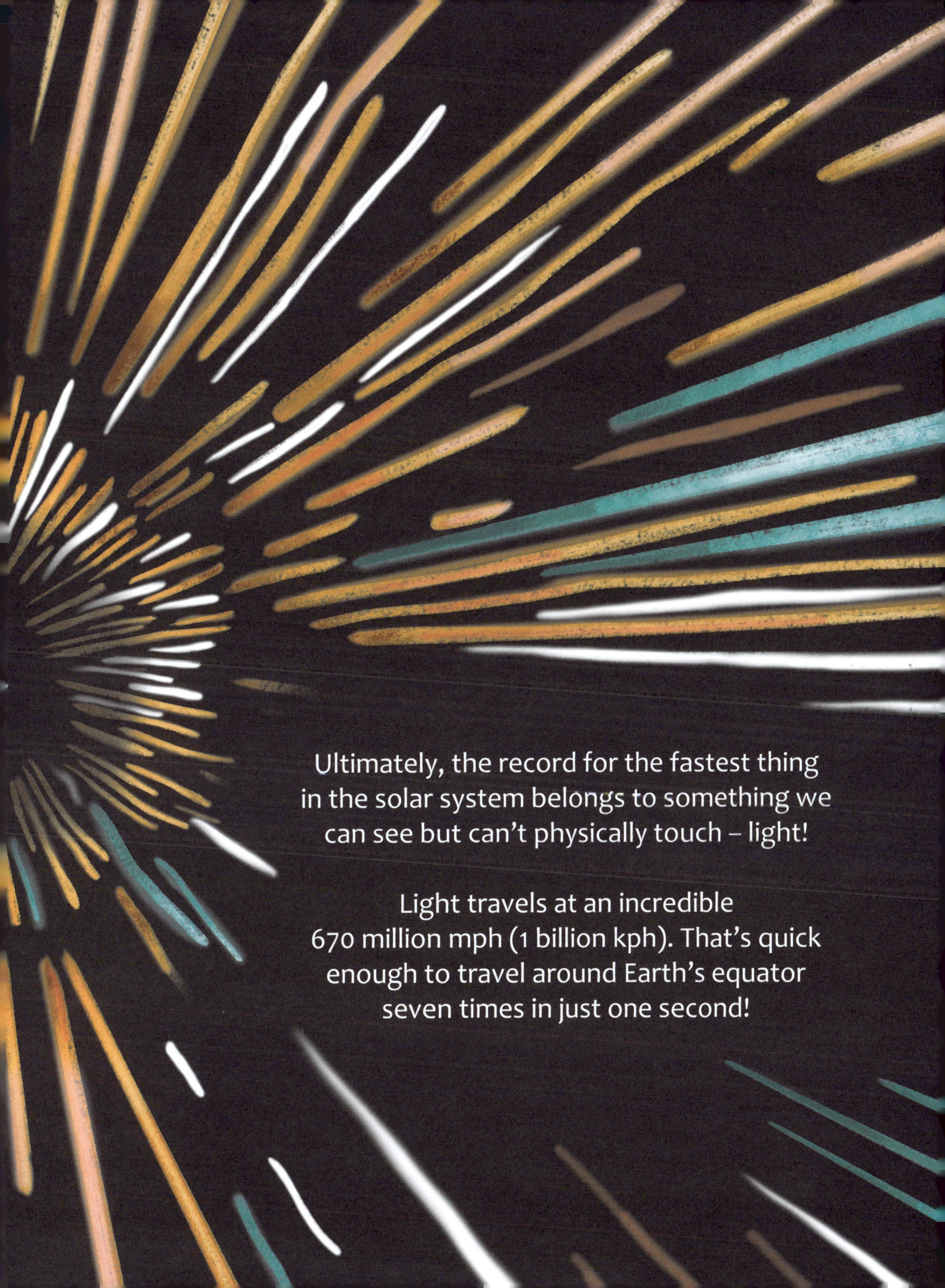

Ultimately, the record for the fastest thing in the solar system belongs to something we can see but can't physically touch – light!

Light travels at an incredible 670 million mph (1 billion kph). That's quick enough to travel around Earth's equator seven times in just one second!

While they may not be the fastest things in outer space, meteors are still very, very quick.

They have fascinated scientists for hundreds of years and will continue to leave their mark on the solar system for hundreds more!

History-making

METEORS

The sight of a "shooting star" blazing across the night's sky is one you are not likely to forget. Some meteors have even gone down in history! Here are some record-breaking space rocks.

LARGEST METEORITE IMPACT

The largest meteorite impact on the Moon that scientists have ever observed was in 2013. It created a flash of light so bright that it could be seen from Earth!

OLDEST METEOR SHOWER

Humans have always watched the night's sky. The first ever recorded sighting of a meteor shower occurred all the way back in 687 BCE – over 2,700 years ago!

LARGEST METEOR SHOWER

The largest meteor showers in history had between 13 and 40 meteors falling each second! The largest meteor showers we regularly see in the present day only have between 50 and 100 in a whole hour.

LARGEST METEORITE

The largest meteorite ever found to have landed on Earth **intact** is called the *Hoba* meteorite. It weighs as much as nine fully-grown African elephants!

MOST EXPENSIVE METEORITE

The most expensive meteorite ever sold was originally found in China in 2000. People paid huge amounts of money for tiny pieces of it that were no heavier than a paper clip.

Mighty

METEOR FACTS

There's so much to discover about the world of meteoritics. Did you know these incredible facts about meteors?

HOME SWEET HOME

1,000 years ago, a small meteorite originally from Mars landed on Earth. In 2021, **NASA**'s Perseverance **rover** returned a small piece of it back home!

KEEP YOUR EYES PEELED

There are several chances each year to watch meteor showers. You don't need a telescope to watch them. All you need are your eyes – and lots of patience!

IT WASN'T A METEOR THAT MADE THE DINOSAURS EXTINCT

It was an asteroid! Asteroids are much bigger and cause a lot more damage, as the dinosaurs unfortunately found out.

BRACE FOR IMPACT

Everything that is launched into space – including the International Space Station, the largest object ever flown in space – has to be shielded from potential meteoroid strikes.

METEOROLOGY ISN'T ABOUT METEORS

A long time ago, the word "meteor" was used to refer to anything in the atmosphere, including clouds, rain, and snow. The study of the weather was therefore called "meteorology".

GLOSSARY

Asteroid – space rocks that orbit (see right) the Sun.

Asteroid belt – an area of the solar system (see right) between Mars and Jupiter where lots of asteroids (see above) can be found.

Atmosphere – the gases that surround a planet.

Craters – dents or holes in the surface of something.

Equator – an invisible line that runs around the middle of Earth, an equal distance from the North and South poles.

Gravity – the force that pulls objects towards each other, keeping planets in orbit (see right) around the Sun and our feet on the ground.

Intact – something that is complete and not damaged.

Kph – kilometers/kilometres per hour.

Meteor shower – an event where multiple meteors can be seen in the night's sky over a short period of time.

Meteorites – small pieces of space rock that have fallen to Earth's surface. *Need help saying this? See below!*

Meteoroids – small pieces of rock floating through space.

Meteors – small pieces of space rock falling through Earth's atmosphere (see left). *Need help saying this? See below!*

Mph – miles per hour.

NASA – the National Aeronautics and Space Administration is an agency that deals with space research and exploration. It's based in the USA.

Orbit – the repeated path taken by one object circling around another object in space.

Rover – a remote-controlled robot built to explore extra-terrestrial planets and moons.

Shielded – to be protected from something.

Solar system – the Sun and everything that moves around it.

Stars – huge, glowing balls made of hot gases. The Sun is the closest star to Earth.

HOW DO I SAY?

Hoba
HOH-bah

Meteor
ME-tee-or

Meteorite
ME-tee-or-ite

Meteoriticists
ME-tee-or-IT-ih-sists

Meteoritics
ME-tee-or-IT-iks

Meteoroid
ME-tee-or-oy-d

THE BIG QUESTIONS ANSWERED

This is more than just a series of books; it is a complete resource. Accompanying each book is a variety of FREE material to engage curious kids with science.

www.thebigquestionsanswered.com

Use the QR code to visit the website, download free resources, and discover other books in the series.

On the website, find out incredible things about meteoriticists, including what they do, some of their greatest discoveries, and the people who have made a difference in this field of science.

The material is also available for home or classroom use, supporting all the information in this book.

Teachers' & Parents' Resources
With discussion prompts, questions, and extra information around key topics.

Activity Pack
Fun activities including creative writing, word searches, and more.

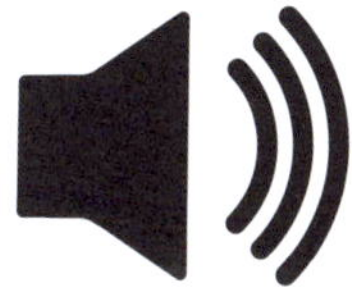

Audio Book
Experience this book in audio, narrated by a professional voice actor.

The Big Questions Answered is published by Beetle Books.
Beetle Books is an imprint of Hungry Tomato Ltd.

First published in 2025 by Hungry Tomato Ltd
F15, Old Bakery Studios, Blewetts Wharf, Malpas Road,
Truro, Cornwall, TR1 1QH, UK.

ISBN 9781835691472

A CIP catalog record for this book is available from the British Library.

With thanks to:
Editors: Jenny Rowan and Holly Thornton
Designers: Meg Holbrook and Amy Harvey
The team at Beehive Illustration
Consultant: Professor Eduard Kontar

Information in this book is up to date as of the time of writing.

Printed and bound in China.

Picture Credits:
(t = top, b = bottom, m = middle, l = left, r = right)
Shutterstock: AstroStar 34bl; Artsiom P 35mr; Bocskai Istvan 33br; Borkin Vadim 35bl; CameraObscura82 32ml; Geermy 33tr; Triff 34mr; ingehogenbijl 33ml; Mikael Damkier 35tl; Vadim Sadovski 32br.